## DATE DUE

| | | |
|---|---|---|
| AP 29 '99 | | |
| MY 13 '99 | | |
| NO 12 '99 | | |
| SEP 2 9 2003 | | |
| NOV 0 7 2003 | | |
| DEC 0 5 2003 | | |
| FEB 1 3 2004 | | |
| NOV 0 7 2004 | | |
| JUN 1 5 2005 | | |
| OCT 0 8 2006 | | |
| NOV 0 1 2006 | | |
| APR 0 6 2007 | | |
| APR 0 6 2007 | | |
| APR 1 8 2007 | | |
| AUG 3 1 2012 | | |
| | | |
| | | |

DEMCO 38-297

BANNOCKBURN SCHOOL DIST. 106
2165 TELEGRAPH ROAD
DEERFIELD, ILLINOIS 60015

W9-ABT-019

# CUTAWAY
# SPACE
# VEHICLES

## JON RICHARDS

**COPPER BEECH BOOKS**
**BROOKFIELD, CONNECTICUT**

BANNOCKBURN SCHOOL DIST.
2165 TELEGRAPH ROAD
DEERFIELD, ILLINOIS 6001

© Aladdin Books Ltd 1998

Designed and
produced by
Aladdin Books Ltd
28 Percy Street
London W1P 0LD

First published in
the United States in 1998 by
Copper Beech Books,
an imprint of
The Millbrook Press
2 Old New Milford Road
Brookfield, Connecticut
06804

Editor
Helen Stone
Consultant
Steve Allman
Design
David West
Children's Book Design
Designer
Robert Perry
Illustrators
Simon Tegg, Alex Pang, &
Richard Rockwood
Picture Research
Brooks Krikler Research

All rights reserved
Printed in Belgium
5 4 3 2 1

Library of Congress
Cataloging-in-Publication Data
Richards, Jon, 1970-
Space vehicles / by Jon Richards;
illustrated by Simon Tegg
p.  cm. — (Cutaway)
Includes index.
Summary : Examines different types of
machines used in space exploration,
including probes, satellites, space
shuttles, and rockets, and describes
the work they do.
ISBN 0-7613-0721-4 (lib. bdg.) —
ISBN 0-7613-0728-1 (trade)
1. Space vehicles—Juvenile literature.
[1. Space vehicles.]
I. Tegg, Simon, ill. II. Title.
III. Series.
TL793.R527  1998        97-47118
629.47—dc21              CIP  AC

# CONTENTS

# INTRODUCTION

It is less than fifty years since we sent the first object out into space. Since then, robot probes have been to nearly every planet in our solar system — a couple have left it altogether and are traveling out to the stars. We have also sent people out of the earth's atmosphere. In specially made space vehicles, they have even been to the moon and back!

**Communications**
These antennae on the front of the space vehicle sent information to mission control (*see* page 11).

**Heat shield**
This protected the capsule and stopped it from burning up when it reentered the atmosphere.

**Instrument panel**
In front of the cosmonaut was a panel of instruments that told him how the space vehicle was performing.

**Reentry vehicle**
After orbiting the earth, the capsule at the front of the space vehicle broke off and returned to Earth with the cosmonaut.

# VOSTOK 1

On April 12, 1961, Yuri A. Gagarin, a Russian cosmonaut, became the first person to leave the earth and go into space.

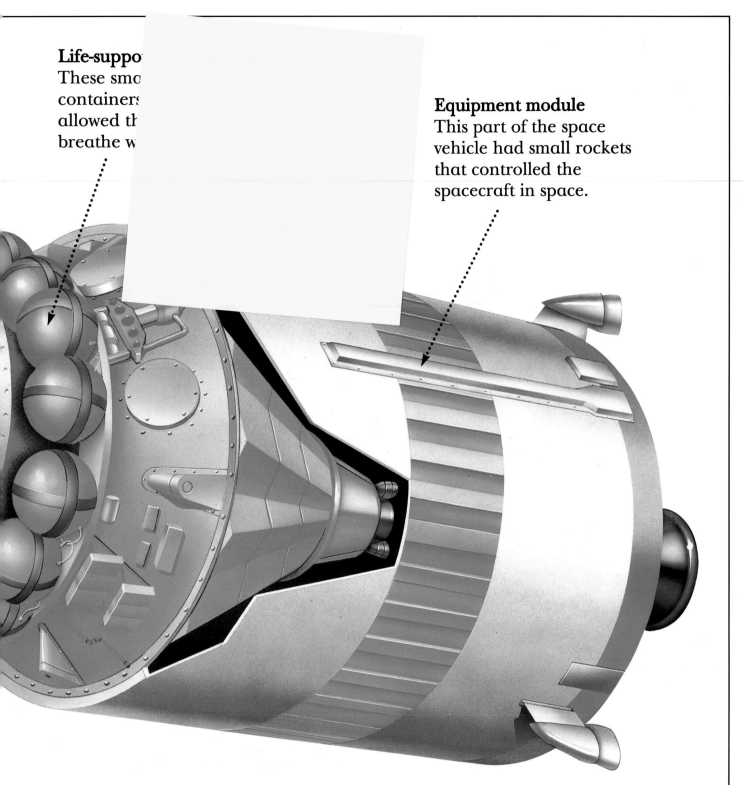

**Life-suppo**
These smo
containers
allowed th
breathe w

**Equipment module**
This part of the space
vehicle had small rockets
that controlled the
spacecraft in space.

He traveled in a spacecraft called *Vostok 1*. This was a small metal vehicle that was fitted to the top of a rocket.

After orbiting, or going around, the earth, he reentered the atmosphere and parachuted safely to the ground.

# Many attempts were

Explosive

Fuel
tank

## Flying bombs
These rockets (*left*) were used toward the end of World War II. They were called V2s. They soared up to the edge of space before diving down onto a target and exploding.

Rocket
engine

## Sputnik
The first object sent into space was a small silver ball called *Sputnik 1* (*left*). It was launched in October 1957. The next month a second spacecraft, *Sputnik 2*, was sent into space. This time it carried a living thing — a small dog named Laika (*right*).

# made to reach space.

## Probing the moon

Many probes have been sent to study the moon. One spacecraft, *Luna 16* (*right*), was sent in September 1970. It gathered samples of rock using a drill and brought them back to Earth.

Drill

Rocket engine

## Gemini

Some of the earliest U.S. astronauts were carried into space in *Gemini* space vehicles (*left*). These capsules could carry two astronauts at a time.

## First stage
The first stage of the *Saturn 5* had five powerful engines that blasted the rocket clear of the launch pad (*see* page 14).

## Fuel tanks
Inside each of the stages were huge tanks of fuel and oxygen. These were mixed in the rocket engines and burned to produce the thrust.

## Third stage
The third and final stage of the *Saturn 5* held the modules that carried the astronauts to the moon.

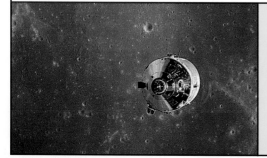

# SATURN 5
One of the most powerful rockets ever built was the *Saturn 5*. This mighty space vehicle carried astronauts to the moon.

## Second stage

The first stage broke away from the rocket when the fuel in its tanks was used up. The rockets in the second stage were then ignited.

## Escape rocket

In an emergency, this would carry the astronauts clear of any danger.

## Moon modules

These small modules sat on top of the *Saturn 5* rocket. The astronauts traveled to the moon inside them (*see* pages 12-13).

It had three sets of rocket engines. These were housed in three separate parts, called stages (*see* page 14).

The *Saturn 5* rocket was very long. If it had been put on its side it would have stretched the length of a football field.

# Rockets are used to

## Firing rockets

The rocket sits silently on the launch pad as the seconds tick down to the launch. Then, when the countdown has finished, the engines ignite (*left*) and push the rocket into the air. BLAST OFF!

## Rocket shapes

Rockets have been built in many different shapes and sizes (*right*). Today, they can carry huge satellites into orbit, or send probes out to the planets.

ЗНЕРГИЯ

US AIR FORCE

# lift things into space.

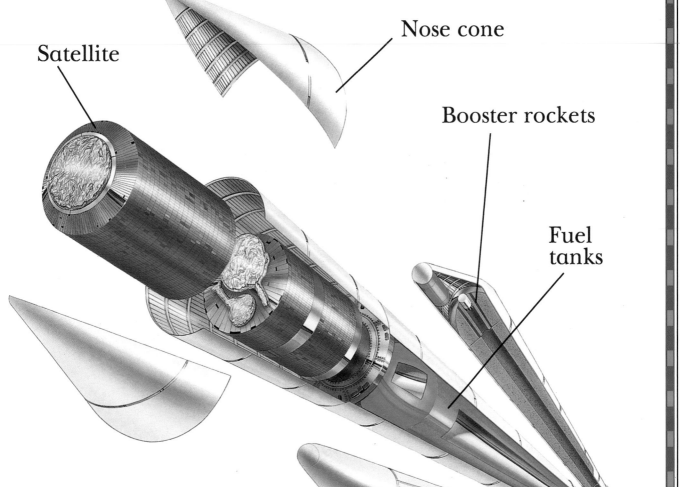

Satellite

Nose cone

Booster rockets

Fuel tanks

## Rocket cargo

A rocket carries its cargo inside its nose cone (*above*). This cargo could be one or two satellites. As it flies through the atmosphere and space, the rocket is guided and watched from mission control (*right*).

**Command module**
This is where the
astronauts sat during
blast-off.

**Service module**
The service module held
the fuel and life-support
systems for the mission to
the moon.

**Control engines**
On the side of each module
were small rocket engines.
These were used to steer the
vehicle through space.

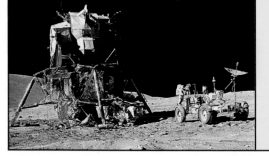

# MOON MODULES

The U.S. astronauts traveled to the moon
inside three space vehicles that were joined
together for most of the journey.

**Lunar module**
Once on the moon, the astronauts left the lunar module to explore the surface.

**Leaving the moon**
This rocket blasted the astronauts clear of the moon's surface and up to the orbiting modules.

**Legs**
When the mission was completed on the surface, the top half of the lunar module blasted clear, leaving the legs on the moon.

These three space vehicles were called the command module, the service module, and the lunar module.

The lunar module carried two astronauts down to the moon, while the third astronaut stayed in orbit around the moon.

# What it took to put

## Blast off

At the end of the countdown, the engines at the the bottom of the *Saturn 5* were ignited. The force from the burning gases pushed the rocket into the atmosphere and toward the moon (*left*).

## Stages

After it had broken away from the *Saturn 5* (*left*), each stage of the rocket fell back to Earth and burned up in the upper atmosphere.

## Moon walk

After they landed on the moon, the astronauts put on special suits to walk on the surface (*left*). Here they collected rocks and carried out experiments.

# people on the moon.

Radio antenna

Camera

## Lunar rover

The lunar rover (*below*) was carried on the side of the lunar module. In this specially designed car, the astronauts could drive far from the module.

Dust guard

Seat

## Splash down

The astronauts returned to Earth inside the command module. After it entered the earth's atmosphere, several parachutes opened to slow the module down. It finally landed in the Pacific Ocean (*right*).

# What it takes to

## Survival training

Astronauts need survival training in case they do not land where they had planned. They could land in the middle of a huge forest or in the wrong part of the sea (*left*).

## Underwater

To cope with being weightless, astronauts practice in swimming pools (*right*). Here they can float freely — just like being in space.

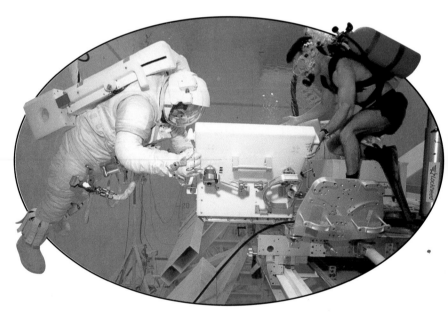

## Floating freely

Astronauts can use a plane to practice being weightless. This flies in a special way that makes those people inside it float freely (*left*). It only lasts a short time, but it can still make people feel ill!

# be an astronaut.

Visor

Camera

Space suit

Controls

## Rocket pack
This rocket pack (*left*) was used by astronauts to fly around without being attached to their spacecraft. It had an air supply to let the astronaut breathe and rockets to push the astronaut around in space.

## Locked up
When the first astronauts came back from the moon they were put in special chambers (*right*). Scientists thought that they might infect humans with germs that might live on the moon.

**Rocket engines**
The shuttle has three main engines. These help to push the spacecraft into the atmosphere along with the powerful rocket boosters (*see* pages 20-21).

**Wings**
The shuttle uses wings to glide through the air after it reenters the atmosphere.

USA

# SPACE SHUTTLE

In 1981 the space shuttle *Columbia* blasted off to become the world's first reusable space vehicle.

## Cargo bay

The shuttle has cargo doors that open to reveal the cargo bay. Here satellites can be carried into orbit or rescued and brought back to Earth for repair.

## Robot arm

The shuttle is fitted with a special robot arm. Astronauts control the arm and use it to launch satellites or bring them into the cargo bay.

## Landing gear

For much of the mission these wheels are folded into the shuttle's nose and wings. Like the wheels of a plane, they are lowered as the shuttle glides in to land.

## Crew's quarters

Up to eight astronauts can live and work in the shuttle's small quarters. These are found behind and beneath the flight deck.

Since then the space shuttles have been used in a huge variety of ways. They have carried satellites into orbit, repaired broken satellites, and docked with space stations. They have also carried out studies into how we could live in space.

# The space shuttle does

## Liftoff

When the space shuttle blasts off it is fitted to two rocket boosters and a big fuel tank (*left*). The boosters are released soon after launch. They parachute back to Earth and are used in a later mission.

## Fixing satellites

Sometimes satellites may need to be repaired. The shuttle can either bring them back down to Earth, or astronauts can fix them while they are still in space (*right*).

BANNOCKBURN SCHOOL DIST. 106
2165 TELEGRAPH ROAD
DEERFIELD, ILLINOIS 60015

# many different jobs.

## Docking

Recently, the shuttle has docked with the Russian space station, *Mir* (*left*). These missions have allowed astronauts to practice for the building of a future space station (*see* pages 26-27).

## Landing

After the shuttle has reentered Earth's atmosphere, it glides down to land at a special airstrip that is near its launch pad (*right*).

## Protective shell

When it entered the atmosphere, the lander was protected by a special shell. This was dropped before the lander touched down.

## Communications

Small antennae on the spacecraft kept it in touch with Earth. They also sent back information and any pictures taken by the probe.

## Fuel tanks

Fuel to power the space probe's small rocket engines was stored in tanks inside the spacecraft.

## VIKING PROBES

In 1976, two probes were sent to Mars. Both called *Viking*, they were each made up of two parts. One part of each probe landed on the planet's surface. The other part stayed in orbit around Mars and sent information back to Earth. Once on the surface, the two landers took many pictures of the landscape. They were also fitted with special tools. These were used to carry out experiments to study the Martian rocks and soil.

**Lander**
When *Viking* reached Mars, the lander was released. It entered the atmosphere and parachuted to the ground. Before it touched down, small rockets fired to slow it even more, and let it land very gently.

**Solar panels**
These convert sunlight into electricity to supply the probe with power during its mission.

# Many probes have

## Galileo

*Galileo* (*right*) traveled to the largest planet in the solar system, Jupiter. It looked at Jupiter's moons and sent a tiny probe into the atmosphere of the giant planet.

Solar panels

## Hubble

This giant telescope (*left*) orbits Earth looking at objects that are very far away. It has been very useful in helping us to understand what happened just after the universe was formed.

Telescope

# been sent into space.

## Pathfinder

*Pathfinder* landed on Mars in 1997. It carried a robot vehicle called *Sojourner* (*right*). This explored the area around the lander and examined rocks and soil on the surface.

## Giotto

Halley's Comet flies past Earth every 76 years. In 1986 a probe called *Giotto* (*left*) was sent to travel into the comet's tail and take pictures of the comet's center.

**Docking**
When spaceships come up from Earth, they will dock at a special port on the space station.

**Laboratories**
Inside these parts of the space station astronauts will carry out many experiments.

**Escape capsule**
In an emergency the astronauts can leave the space station in a special capsule and return safely to Earth.

# SPACE STATION

The International Space Station will be built by countries from all over the world, including the U.S.A., Russia, and Japan.

**Structure**
The space station will be too big to take into space in one piece. Instead, parts will be carried up in stages and put together while in orbit.

**Living quarters**
Although the living quarters are small, seven astronauts will be able to live in them.

**Solar panels**
These will need to be massive to supply the space station with all the energy it will use.

It will orbit high above Earth, and people will live and work inside. It will also show how well humans can live in space.

In the future, the astronauts may be carried up to the space station by the next generation of space shuttles.

# Living in space causes

## Eating

Because everything is weightless in space, astronauts eat food from specially made containers and tubes (*above*). Otherwise the food would float around in a gooey mess!

## Exercise

Because they can float around in space without any effort, astronauts need to exercise (*right*). If they did not their muscles would waste away and they would have trouble walking when they returned to Earth.

# a lot of problems.

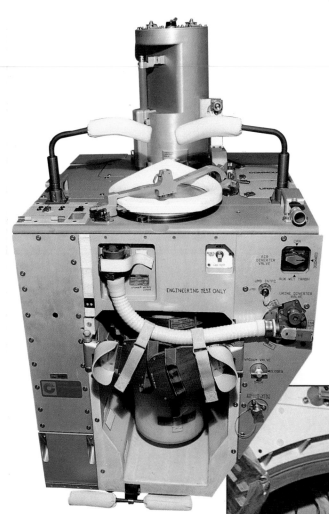

## Space toilet
Going to the bathroom in space can cause problems! To overcome this scientists have built a special toilet (*left*) to let astronauts go without causing a mess.

## Washing
Specially designed washing facilities help astronauts keep themselves clean — without getting the rest of the spacecraft wet (*right*)!

# Fantastic facts

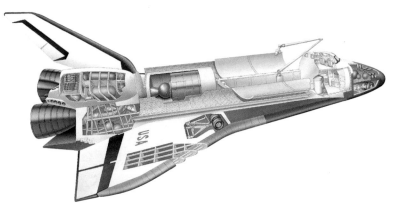

• The most powerful rocket ever built was the Russian NI booster. Launched in 1969, it exploded just 70 seconds after blast-off.

• The space probe *Pioneer 10* is currently the farthest artificial object sent into space. It passed beyond the orbit of Pluto in 1986 and is now nearly 6 billion miles (10 billion km) away from Earth.

• The Hubble Space Telescope is the largest telescope in space. It weighs more than two fully grown elephants!

• The *Pathfinder* probe that landed on Mars in 1997 was fitted with the most powerful computer to go into space. This was capable of handling 22 million instructions every second!

# Space words

## Astronaut

A person who travels into space. Russian astronauts are called cosmonauts.

## Atmosphere

A layer of gases that covers a planet. The atmosphere around Earth allows us to live.

## Docking

The process in which vehicles join together. Docking in space can be very tricky!

## Heat shield

A protective layer on a space vehicle. It stops the craft from burning up when it enters a planet's atmosphere.

## Orbit

A path around another body. The moon orbits the earth, while the earth orbits the sun.

## Probe

A spacecraft that is sent to study other planets and stars.

## Space station

A large spacecraft that remains in orbit around the earth. Astronauts live and work inside it, sometimes for very long periods.

## Stage

Rockets are made up of stages. Each stage has its own fuel supply and engines.

# Index

PHOTO CREDITS
Abbreviations: t-top, m-middle, b-bottom, r-right, l-left, c-center.

All the pictures in this book are from NASA except the following pages;
pages 4 & 26 – Frank Spooner Pictures. 6 & 16t – Novosti.
23 – Science Photo Library.